W9-BKV-326

FOOTBALL LEGENDS

Terry Bradshaw

Jim Brown

Joe Montana

Joe Namath

Walter Payton

Jerry Rice

CHELSEA HOUSE PUBLISHERS

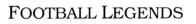

JOE NAMATH

Bruce Chadwick

Introduction by
Chuck Noll

CHELSEA HOUSE PUBLISHERS
New York • Philadelphia

Produced by Daniel Bial and Associates
New York, New York.

Picture research by Alan Gottlieb
Cover illustration by Charles Lilly

Copyright © 1995 by Chelsea House Publishers, a division of Main Line
Book Co. All rights reserved. Printed and bound in the United States of
America.

3 5 7 9 8 6 4 2

Chadwick, Bruce.
    Joe Namath / Bruce Chadwick.
      p.   cm. — (Football legends)
    Includes bibliographical references (p.   ) and index.
    ISBN 0-7910-2454-7
    1. Namath, Joe Willie, 1943–   —Juvenile literature. 2. Football
players—United States—Biography—Juvenile literature. 3. National
Football League—Juvenile literature. [1. Namath, Joe Willie, 1943–
2. Football players.] I. Title. II. Series.
    GV939.N28C43 1994
    796.332'092—dc20
    [B]   94-1351
                                                              CIP
                                                               AC

CONTENTS

A WINNING ATTITUDE

Chuck Noll

Don't ever fall into the trap of believing, "I could never do that. And I won't even try—I don't want to embarrass myself." After all, most top athletes had no idea what they could accomplish when they were young. A secret to the success of every star quarterback and sure-handed receiver is that they tried. If they had not tried, if they had not persevered, they would never have discovered how far they could go and how much they could achieve.

You can learn about trying hard and overcoming challenges by being a sports fan. Or you can take part in organized sports at any level, in any capacity. The student messenger at my high school is now president of a university. A reserve ballplayer who got very little playing time in high school now owns a very successful business. Both of them benefited by the lesson of perseverance that sports offers. The main point is that you don't have to be a Hall of Fame athlete to reap the benefits of participating in sports.

In math class, I learned that the whole is equal to the sum of its parts. But that is not always the case when you are dealing with people. Sports has taught me that the whole is either greater than or less than the sum of its parts, depending on how well the parts work together. And how the parts work together depends on how they really understand the concept of teamwork.

Most people believe that teamwork is a fifty-fifty proposition. But true teamwork is seldom, if ever, fifty-fifty. Teamwork is *whatever it takes to get the job done.* There is no time for the measurement of contributions, no time for anything but concentrating on your job.

One year, my Pittsburgh Steelers were playing the Houston Oilers in the Astrodome late in the season, with the division championship on the line. Our offensive line was hard hit by the flu, our starting quarterback was out with an injury, and we were having difficulty making a first down. There was tremendous pressure on our defense to perform well—and they rose to the occasion. If the players on the defensive unit had been measuring their contribution against the offense's contribution, they would have given up and gone home. Instead, with a "whatever it takes" attitude, they increased their level of concentration and performance, forced turnovers, and got the ball into field goal range for our offense. Thanks to our defense's winning attitude, we came away with a victory.

Believing in doing whatever it takes to get the job done is what separates a successful person from someone who is not as successful. Nobody can give you this winning outlook; you have to develop it. And I know from experience that it can be learned and developed on the playing field.

My favorite people on the football field have always been offensive linemen and defensive backs. I say this because it takes special people to perform well in jobs in which there is little public recognition when they are doing things right but are thrust into the spotlight as soon as they make a mistake. That is exactly what happens to a lineman whose man sacks the quarterback or a defensive back who lets his receiver catch a touchdown pass. They know the importance of being part of a group that believes in teamwork and does not point fingers at one another.

Sports can be a learning situation as much as it can be fun. And that's why I say, "Get involved. Participate."

CHUCK NOLL, the Pittsburgh Steelers head coach from 1969–1991, led his team to four Super Bowl victories—the most by any coach. Widely respected as an innovator on both offense and defense, Noll was inducted into the Pro Football Hall of Fame in 1993.

1

UNDERDOGS

More than 75,000 people walked slowly into the Orange Bowl, in Miami, Florida, for Super Bowl III in January 1969. The fans took their time parking their cars in lots surrounded by palm trees, buying souvenirs, and eating lunch at the dozens of busy concession stands that dotted the stadium which hosts the famous bowl game of the same name in college football each year. The fans, most in short sleeves, climbed the high steps of the Orange Bowl slowly, in no hurry to reach their seats. After all, everyone knew the game was going to be a blowout.

The Super Bowl was a game dreamed up as a first step to a merger between the American Football League (AFL) and the National Football League (NFL), a title game between the champs

Bubba Smith of the Baltimore Colts (number 78)—all 6'7" of him—leaps, trying to block Joe Namath's pass attempt. Namath, though, could not be stopped, and the New York Jets won perhaps the most important Super Bowl Game ever played, 16-7.

of each league. The NFL had dominated the first two matchups as the Green Bay Packers destroyed the Kansas City Chiefs in 1967 and the Oakland Raiders in 1968. Critics said the game should not be played anymore because the NFL clubs were obviously superior. Even the biggest fans of the AFL were daunted at how easily the Packers had beaten their teams.

The effectiveness of Matt Snell's running in the 1969 Super Bowl allowed Namath to attempt fewer passes than usual.

The NFL champs in the 1969 game were the mighty Baltimore Colts, a team which had lost only two games in the last two years. They were so good that they had won the NFL title in a 34-0 rout of the Cleveland Browns. The New York Jets, meanwhile, had barely beaten the Raiders in the AFL title game.

Joe Namath, the Jets' star quarterback, had suffered a bad back, mangled fingers, and a possible concussion in the Raider game, to go along with his longstanding knee problems. Meanwhile, the Colts' starting quarterback, Earl Morrall, had just been voted the NFL Player of the Year, and his backup was the legendary Johnny Unitas.

The Colts' backfield included Tom Matte, the short, strong, running back. Wide receiver Jimmy Orr was one of the best, and the tight end, John Mackey, was All Pro and a future Hall of Famer. The defensive line, with Fred

Mitchell and Bubba Smith, was huge and mean. The oddsmakers quickly installed the Colts as the biggest favorites in Super Bowl history, saying they would win by 17 points. They later upped the spread to 21 points. Some writers were saying privately that the Colts could win by as many as 40. The Jets were one of the biggest underdogs in the history of all sports.

Another lopsided AFL loss in Super Bowl III might mean the end of the new league. In the 1940s, the All American Conference had tried to compete with the NFL but folded after a few years. By 1969, the AFL had survived for eight seasons, and its team owners, coaches, and players felt they were close to forcing a merger with the older league. After two straight losses in the Super Bowl, though, sportswriters thought that another blowout could be devastating to the AFL's chances of survival.

None of this bothered young Joe Namath, the Jets' colorful quarterback, who had made front-page news around the world just four years before, when he signed with the Jets for $427,000, the highest salary in the history of football up to that time. The cocky Namath laughed when told the early point spread was 17. "Hey, that's ridiculous," he said. "We shouldn't be favored by more than eight or nine."

When asked about Earl Morrall of the Colts, Joe scoffed. "We've got four quarterbacks better than him in our own league," he said. "John Hadl of the [San Diego] Chargers, Daryle Lamonica of the [Oakland] Raiders, Bob Griese of the [Miami] Dolphins, and myself."

This kind of talk outraged fans. It was forbidden in the world of professional athletics. The

Earl Morrall of the Colts couldn't lead his team to a score; Verlon Biggs (number 86) of the Jets, though, was an emotional leader of his team.

star was always supposed to be contrite and humble. Opponents were to be taken seriously and with respect.

Joe didn't back down. When he got to Florida, he continued his criticisms. Don Shula, the Colts' young and innovative head coach, was furious. "How Namath can rap Earl is a thing I don't understand. How do you rap a guy who's NFL Player of the Year?"

Many players think they'll win a game, but don't say so in public. It just isn't done. Not Joe Namath, nicknamed Broadway Joe by the New York press for his late-night habits. He wanted the whole world to know the Jets were going to win. At a dinner attended by many in the media just a few days before the Super Bowl, he looked over the large audience and said, "The Jets will win Sunday. I guarantee it!"

The cocky quarterback had crossed the line. The writers mumbled: He would pay on the field. After all, Fred Williamson, the Kansas City defensive lineman, had warned the Packers of his tackling fame before a previous Super Bowl, and the Packers responded by hitting Williamson so hard he was carried off the field on a stretcher.

In his autobiography, Namath defended his mouth. "I wasn't too impressed with the Baltimore defense. Come to think of it, judging from a couple of their games I saw on television, I wasn't too impressed with their offense, either. And I felt that we had a stronger team physically. Almost all of us were under 30, and a lot of us were 24 and 25 and 26. Yet, because we started with the Jets when the Jets were down, we had just as much playing experience as the older Colts. I bet I'd thrown almost as many passes in four seasons as Earl Morrall had thrown in 13."

When the talking stopped and the game began, Baltimore was enraged. But the Jets came out fast and tough. On the second play of the game, Matt Snell carried the ball and collided with Rich Volk of the Colts. Volk was carried off the field with a concussion. The Jets' drive stalled, and Baltimore roared back with a drive to the Jet 31 yardline. Lou Michaels tried a field goal; it missed.

And so it went. Namath threw a 50-yard bomb to Don Maynard, who had shot down the sideline and was in the clear; the ball fell off his fingertips. Morrall drove the Colts to the Jet 12 yardline and fired a pass that cornerback Al Atkinson deflected in the end zone and Randy Beverly intercepted close to the ground for a touchback. The Colts had been stopped again.

Unlike most of today's quarterbacks, Namath called all of the offense's plays. Now he called three running plays in a row. The Colts, certain he would pass on the next play, rushed hard. Namath dropped back, then handed off to Snell, who picked up 12 yards on the draw.

Back in the huddle, Namath barked, "Play at line," meaning he would call the play when he saw how the Colts lined up. (Half the Jets' plays were called at the line.) He liked what he saw. The Colts, now scared of Maynard on the left side, shaded their defense that way, leaving the right side open for George Sauer. Namath promptly called Sauer's number and hit him for 14 yards, then for 11.

Emerson Boozer carried twice to the Colts' 21 yardline. Certain Namath would throw into the end zone, the Colts blitzed. Namath waited until the last second and then dumped a short pass at the line of scrimmage, right over the blitzers' heads, for a 12-yard gain. A few plays later, Snell ran off tackle for a touchdown, and the Jets led 7-0. It was the first time an AFL team ever had a lead in the Super Bowl.

The Jets' Johnny Sample picked off another Morrall pass in the end zone, and Jim Hudson also made an interception just before the half-time gun. A thrilled Jets team carried the 7-0 lead into the lockerroom.

Tom Matte fumbled on the first play of the second half. The Jets recovered, and Jim Turner kicked a 32-yard field goal. A few minutes later, Namath hit Maynard at the back of the end zone for what appeared to be a touchdown, but the referee ruled Maynard was over the back line and disallowed the score. Turner booted another field goal, and the Jets moved ahead 13-0.

Shula put in Unitas late in the game, and Johnny U. did engineer a touchdown near the end. But the Jets won, 16-7, turning the football world upside down. Joe Namath had completed 17 of 28 passes for 206 yards, with no interceptions (then a record). But statistics never tell the whole story. He had led his team with the poise of a veteran in guiding them to perhaps the greatest upset in the history of football. And he had proved that the players in the AFL were as good as those in the NFL.

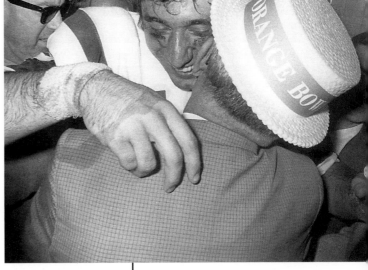

A tired but happy Joe Namath gets a hug from his father in the lockerroom after Super Bowl III.

Namath wound up setting several records for yards passing. He was the first quarterback to throw for nearly 500 yards in a single game, the first to throw for 4,000 yards in a single season. Playing on bad knees that would have sidelined most players, he was an inspiration to those who knew him.

When all the 400-yard games and six-touchdown games are forgotten, though, and when the championship rings gather dust, Joe Namath will still be remembered as the man who had the courage to tell the world that nobody could beat his team and the man who, with that victory, singlehandedly forced the merger of the two leagues into the NFL we know today.

2
BEAVER FALLS JOE

Like many great athletes, Joe Namath was so gifted he could play several sports well as a boy. There was little difference to him if his large hands were passing a football, shooting a basketball, or throwing a baseball. Some young athletes are so good they develop into professional stars in two sports, like Bo Jackson and Deion Sanders, or succeed in one sport after a career in another, like pro golfers John Brodie and Ralph Terry. Some choose one sport over another, like Ryne Sandberg, the recent Chicago Cubs second baseman, who was a great high school quarterback. When Joe Namath was still a teenager, he was just as good at basketball (14 points per game) and baseball (.450 batting average) as he was at football. He had that rare natural ability to play different sports and be graceful at each.

But like some other superstars in their early years, Joe Namath's ability wasn't quickly recog-

Joe Namath (number 24) starred in basketball and baseball as well as football in high school.

nized. Like the basketball coaches in North Carolina who cut Michael Jordan from his high school team because they felt he wasn't talented enough, Namath's high school football coaches didn't realize his skills until it was almost too late.

Joseph William Namath was born on May 31, 1943, and grew up in Beaver Falls, Pennsylvania. His family lived in a racially mixed, lower-middle-class section of town near several of the large smoke-belching steel mills that were the heartbeat of Beaver Falls' economy. Joe was one of the five children of John and Rose Namath. Joe's father and grandfather, who emigrated to the U.S. from Hungary, both worked in the grimy steel mills all their lives, coming home tired and weary every night.

Beaver Falls, like many towns in western Pennsylvania, was crazy for football. The area has produced an inordinate number of football stars over the years, including Babe Parilli, Mike Ditka, Tony Dorsett, Joe Montana, Terry Hanratty, Joe Walton, and Dan Marino. The boys went into football at their parents urging because success on the gridiron was the fastest avenue out of a life in the steel mills. Success on the field meant college scholarships. Joe's three older brothers all played high school football, and one, Frank, played at the University of Kentucky.

Ironically, all were physically more adept than Joe as teenagers. Joe had huge hands and strong legs, but he was not tall, very thin, and gangling. In grade school, he was so small that he couldn't see over any of the kids on his pee-wee football team who blocked for him. He went completely unnoticed in ninth grade and was an unheralded junior varsity quarterback as a sophomore. He didn't move up to the varsity until the last game of his sophomore year. As a junior, and still just 5′ 10″ and 150 pounds, he was a backup for most of the season and alternated as a starter only during the last few games on a lackluster team.

He played well those last few games of 1959, though, and the high school's new coach, Larry Bruno, noticed something else. Namath had a swagger about him. He was a buccaneer as a quarterback—bold and daring. He forced passes no one else would, took off on option runs through holes most would avoid, threw deep passes into heavy coverage, and completed them. In September 1960, Joe's senior year, Bruno named him the team's starting quarterback—and punter—for what most thought would be another mediocre season.

Over the summer Joe had shot up to 6′ 2″ and put on 25 pounds. He now had a clear vision of the entire field when he dropped back to pass. Despite his increased size, Joe could run faster and react more quickly. Nowadays, if a high school athlete shot up this much, people would wonder if he had taken steroids. But in 1960, steroids were totally unknown in western Pennsylvania. Joe's growth spurt was natural.

Local writers didn't have to wait long to see if Namath could handle the starting job. On the second play of the opening game, against Midland High School, he faked a handoff and sprinted around right end for a 60-yard touchdown. He later scored on an off-tackle run. As a passer, he was 7 of 17 for 174 yards, and Beaver Falls won, 43-13. In the second game, Namath threw a touchdown pass in the game's opening minutes and finished the day 8 of 9 as Beaver

Namath's high school yearbook proclaimed he was a "magician with a football" and "carefree."

Despite the small size of Beaver Falls, PA, Namath led its varsity football team to a perfect record during his senior year.

Falls rolled over Sharon High, 39-7. Joe hurt his leg just before the third game and was asked if he could still punt. In a reply which was to set the tone for his NFL brashness, he told his coach, "Don't worry. It won't be necessary to kick." He was right. Beaver Falls beat a tough New Castle team, from a school three times as big as Beaver Falls, 39-0.

Against undefeated Ambridge, rated one of the top teams in the country, he showed his toughness. Early in the game he separated his shoulder. Slowed by the injury, he still led the Fallsmen to victory. The shoulder was worse the next week, but Joe begged Bruno to get him into the game somehow. Bruno sent him to an orthopedic specialist who taped Namath's shoulder. Joe was 11 of 18, throwing for two touchdowns and running for another two as the team won again.

They never lost. Tiny Beaver Falls startled everyone by going undefeated. Namath completed 85 of 146 for 1,564 yards and 12 touchdowns for a team that used a basic running offense. He ran for six touchdowns and had four called back. It was the opening chapter of a long career.

Namath, always the rebel, had his scrapes with authority in high school, but those who knew him say that people and the press blew most of them out of proportion. There was the flagpole incident. Joe was so elated after one victory that he climbed the flagpole in front of the local Chevrolet showroom and had to be coaxed down by the police. There was the basketball game incident. Joe and his buddies often sneaked into basketball games when they were in junior high. He became so bold about it that he challenged a cop to catch him. The cop did. Then there was the near arrest for trespassing. Everybody used to sneak into the school gym to shoot baskets when it was locked. Joe was the one the police caught. Everything seemed to be taken the wrong way because Namath was a teenaged star. It added to his rebel legend.

Scouts watched most of his games, drooling, and at the end of the year he had 52 scholarship offers from colleges and an offer to play professional baseball for Kansas City. He seriously considered Notre Dame University but dismissed it when he learned it was, at the time, an all-boys school. He was urged by many people to play for Bear Bryant at the University of Alabama, so he and a friend paid a visit to the Bear that spring.

They seemed complete opposites. Bryant was a Deep South conservative with strict disciplinary personal habits and a symbol of authority. The day they met, Namath arrived with his hair long under a wild looking straw hat with a band around it and a toothpick casually sticking out of the side of his mouth. In his looks and life-style, he was as much the rebel from up north as the Bear was the traditional figure of southern respectability. Bryant invited Namath up to the high tower from which he supervised practice (few were extended that invitation). In a 30-minute talk, he told Joe bluntly that he wanted him because he was a winner and the Bear was a winner. Joe chose to sign on with Coach Bryant.

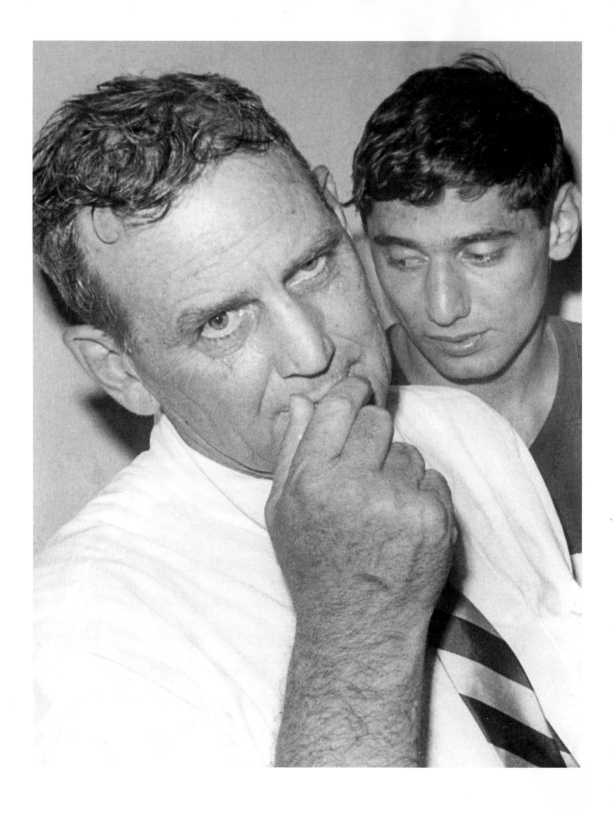

3

JOE AND THE BEAR

Practices were long and hard at the University of Alabama. Of 55 freshmen in 1961, only 11 returned to play football the next year. Namath did not like the long drills. He didn't like living so far away from home. He didn't like southern segregation and racism. He didn't fit in. His classmates dressed conservatively while Joe wore his hair long, topped by a red beret. He had little use for the gentility of southern life. He was so unhappy he seriously considered taking a $50,000 bonus from the Baltimore Orioles to play baseball. Bear Bryant and others talked him into staying, though, and made him Alabama's starting quarterback as a sophomore on an injury-ravaged team which, like his high school squad, was expected to go nowhere.

Bryant loved Joe's ability to run or throw and his incredibly quick release of the ball from his large, sure hands. In the nearly four decades since Namath's college debut, only Dan Marino

Joe Namath and Coach Bear Bryant had strongly different personalities—but they were both winners.

of the Miami Dolphins has matched his quick release. That fast release always gave Namath an extra millisecond to find an open receiver.

"There were very few adjustments that he had to make," Bryant said of Namath's move from high school to college. "He was a polished athlete. All he had to do was discipline himself to our game plan."

Namath's second pass at Alabama went to end Richard Williamson for a touchdown. Later, he threw two more touchdown passes, tying a school record, and went 10 of 14 and ran for 36 yards. This was all in his first varsity game. The Crimson Tide rolled over a tough University of Georgia team that day, 35-0.

Alabama won its next seven games. In a 36-3 victory over the University of Miami, Joe averaged 11 yards a carry as a runner. Alabama lost to Georgia Tech the next week but bounced back to beat Auburn University and went on to a 17-0 victory over Oklahoma University in the 1962 Orange Bowl. Namath set numerous quarterback records as he led Alabama to a number five national ranking.

Namath had another good season as a junior, although his passing and rushing numbers were below those of the previous year. He hoped to redeem himself in the final game against Miami. But sometime after the previous week's loss to Auburn, Namath was seen breaking Bryant's strict training rules. (Rumor had it he was drinking). Bryant confronted him and asked him if the reports were true. Namath admitted it. Bryant was determined to show the team that no one player, no matter how brilliant, could flout the rules. He called a press conference and announced he was suspending his superstar

25

JOE AND THE BEAR

Playing despite great pain, Namath threw two touchdowns in the second half of the 1965 Orange Bowl to bring Alabama back into the game against Texas.

quarterback for the remainder of the season.

"I knew Joe wasn't a bad boy," Bryant later said. "I don't think he became bigheaded and felt he was above training rules. I don't think he was ever bigheaded—just always confident, and I like that. I feel if I'd done a good job of leadership, the suspension wouldn't have happened."

Namath, who had been able to do pretty much whatever he wanted all of his life, was astounded but took the punishment without complaining. Later, Namath would say the suspension was the big turning point in his life. "It was the roughest thing I've had to face," Joe said. "It helped me grow up. One of the assets in playing for Coach Bryant is that he teaches you a lot of things besides football. He's not just a coach. He makes a man out of you. You learn how to act and you learn some things about life."

Namath sat on the sidelines and watched as Steve Sloan, who would be a fine pro quarterback himself, led the team to a win over Miami and a Sugar Bowl championship.

Joe arrived for spring practice in 1964 a changed man. Oh, the swagger was till there. The confidence in himself was there. The Joe Namath rebellion was still there (he even grew a small goatee). But he arrived as a man who was learning from his mistakes, a man who realized he had to change his ways. It was obvious from the first day of spring drills.

"Before, Joe used to do his job and expect everyone else to do theirs," said one of his teammates. "This year he's after everybody all the way. You can see the team pick up when he comes in."

There was some grumbling. If Namath had been suspended—punished—why was he being rewarded with the starting job? And a common complaint in the Deep and tradition-oriented South was, Why was Namath continuing to wear his hair long and sport flashy clothes? Why was he allowed to showboat?

Joe paid little attention to the complaints, and Bear Bryant paid none. Joe's aggressive new leadership was evident in the first three games of his senior year. Against Georgia, Joe completed 16 of 21 passes for 167 yards and ran for three touchdowns in a 31-3 rout. The next week he hit 10 of 20 for two touchdowns against Tulane University in a 33-0 drubbing. He hit 13 of 23 for two touchdowns the next week in a 24-0 shutout of Vanderbilt University.

Then came the North Carolina State University game, a day that changed Joe Namath's life forever. As he dressed, he decided not to tape his shoes to his ankles as he usually did. All players wore black sneakers, but the white tape made his look white. People had accused Joe of donning white shoes simply as a sign of flash. Actually, Joe's main reason for using the tape was to support his ankles. But on this day, he put the tape aside.

Namath got off to a brilliant start, as usual. He hit 7 of 8 passes in the first 15 minutes.

Then he sprinted right on an option play and cut left. Suddenly, his knee gave out, and he collapsed on the field. He couldn't get up. Medics rushed him off the field and spent the rest of the game working on his knee. Early the next day, it was swollen badly and full of fluid. Throughout the remainder of the season, doctors had to use long, thick needles to drain fluid out of the knee. He managed to play most of the remaining games on the schedule, but he had little movement as a runner and weak support in his knees when he positioned himself to pass.

Joe came off the bench to complete 4 of 8 passes to beat Georgia Tech. He was 6 of 9 with a touchdown to beat Auburn and give Alabama a bid to the Orange Bowl and the nation's number one ranking. Bad knee and all, Joe completed 64 of 100 passes for six touchdowns for the year. Then, a week before the Orange Bowl against the University of Texas, his knee collapsed in practice. He couldn't play.

Texas knew a win would give it the national championship. The Longhorns, relying on a running attack led by big Ernie Koy, rolled to an easy 14-0 lead. Sloan was unable to get Alabama on the scoreboard. Bryant asked Namath if it was possible for him to play. Joe put on his helmet and trotted onto the field.

Namath completed six passes in a row to put Alabama on the board. Despite the dreadful pain in his knee, he completed 18 of 37 passes for 255 yards and two touchdowns. With a minute to go, Texas stopped a fourth-down Namath plunge at the three yardline to hold on to a 23-17 victory. Sportswriters, who saw how bad Namath's knee was before the game, said it was one of the gutsiest performances they ever saw.

4

BROADWAY JOE

Pro football was in a war in the winter of 1965. The American Football League, formed in 1960, had gone head to head with the long-established National Football League for five years without much success. The old NFL had tradition, fans, media, and money behind it. The newly formed AFL did not have tradition or much media support, but with a high-scoring, wild, wide-open pass-oriented style of play, it was drawing fans. By 1965, though, even with stars like Daryle Lamonica, Bob Griese, and John Hadl, it had been unable to rival the successful NFL. It was still considered second rate, and sportswriters began to wonder if the AFL would last.

Joe Namath's performance in the Orange Bowl impressed everybody, but most of all it impressed David "Sonny" Werblin, former president

Would Joe Namath be worth the huge salary offered by the New York Jets? Absolutely. In a game against the Houston Oilers in 1966, he threw for five touchdowns, including one on this play to Don Maynard.

of MCA, Inc., a huge record and entertainment company. In the winter of 1965, Werblin, the owner of the New York Jets, was certain that Joe Namath would make the Jets AFL champions. He was also certain, from years of dealing with music and movie personalities (many of them unknowns whom he made prominent with his promotional genius), that Namath had the charm and charisma to be more than a great football player—he could be a star. Werblin was certain that Namath's bold personality, rebellious style, and good looks would make him the most famous athlete in America and vault the AFL over the NFL or into a long-sought merger.

Werblin had so much faith in Namath that, after a money war with the St. Louis Cardinals of the NFL, he signed Joe to the biggest salary contract in the history of football up to that time—a three-year deal worth $427,000. The deal made splashy front-page headlines all over America and was the number one topic of conversation among sports fans for months. The contract itself, and the enormous publicity it started, seemed to vault the struggling AFL up a few notches toward equality with the NFL. Late-night talk show hosts and comedians from coast to coast put routines about Joe Namath and his money into their acts. Many were critical of the deal. Why so much money for an untested rookie with bad knees? Why give him much more than established stars?

Friends of Werblin tell this story. Skeptics, uncertain of Werblin's faith in Namath, were told to meet Sonny at a famous New York restaurant for dinner one night at 8 p.m. They sat at his table for an hour and turned as he pointed out the different major political figures, athletes, and movie stars who walked into the main dining room. Each received some attention, but not much, from the diners. At nine o'clock, Joe Namath walked in. Every head in the restaurant turned, and people at different tables asked for his autograph as he walked toward Werblin.

"All those people are merely famous," Werblin said to his friends, waving at the notables dining. "Joe Namath is a star!"

Namath's arrival at the Jets training camp in the summer of 1965 was greeted with anticipation by the press. He would be under tremendous pressure throughout his rookie season to prove to the writers and fans that he was worth the money. There would be little pressure from the one source he feared most, though—his new teammates.

"We had all seen him play on television. We had followed him in the papers and on TV since he was a sophomore at Alabama. He was very well publicized. We all knew that he had the ingredients to be a great pro quarterback," said Don Maynard, already a five-year NFL and AFL veteran and the Jets' top receiver when Namath arrived. "He was tall, strong, quick on his feet, even with his knee troubles, and had a quick release. He could throw long and short.

"Make it?" Maynard continued. "We all knew Joe Namath would make it. There was absolutely no skepticism about his ability from the players. Not from anybody."

In the summer of 1965, New York was not a football town. It was a baseball town. The New York Yankees had won 15 pennants and 10 World Series in the last 18 years and finished first the last five years in a row. Although the brand new Mets were a terrible baseball team, in

1965 they had a loyal following of fans. Football was the runner up. No New York football team had its own stadium. The New York Giants leased Yankee Stadium on Sundays in the fall and the Jets leased Shea Stadium, which had just opened. (The Jets, first known as the Titans, had played several years in the 50-year-old, run-down Polo Grounds).

The tradition-rich New York Giants felt they had little to fear from the upstart Jets. The Giants had played in the NFL since its founding in the 1920s. They played in the very first NFL championship game in 1933. Since then, they had played in more NFL title games, 14, than any other team. The Giants were one of the best teams in the NFL in the early 1960s, with superstars like Y. A. Tittle, Kyle Rote, Frank Gifford, and Sam Huff, and played in three straight NFL championships.

Namath rests his injured knee in his New York City apartment after the 1967 season. The quarterback spent the then-princely sum of $25,000 decorating his bachelor pad, which featured a full-length llama rug.

All Joe Namath had to do was win an AFL title, bring the league into the spotlight, win New York fans over from baseball to football, and deflect attention from the powerful Giants.

As soon as Joe arrived in New York he found his name appeared in the gossip columns as often as the sports columns. With his contract money, he rented an apartment in one of the poshest sections of town and spent $25,000 decorating it. He bought a huge circular bed and a six-inch-thick white llama rug as centerpieces of the apartment. Pictures of the bed found their way into many newspapers and magazines. He began traveling the night-club circuit and was seen with dozens of beautiful girls. Clubs where he hung out, such as Mr. Laffs, had to turn away hundreds of people each evening. Namath quickly developed a reputation as a girl-crazy, playboy quarterback who loved to see his name in the papers. The press soon dubbed him "Broadway Joe." Football had never seen anything like him.

Could he play pro football, though? And what about his health? Surgery was performed on the knee in the winter, and the doctors pronounced it as good as new, but would it hold up under the relentless rush of linemen? Head coach Weeb Ewbank, a tough, roly-poly taskmaster whose crewcut grey hair was as short as Joe's was long, was pleased with Namath's play in preseason games but did not want to rush him. Namath sat on the bench the entire first game, in Houston, watching Mike Taliaferro hit just 4 of 22 passes in a loss. Things changed the next week, though, at home, in Shea Stadium. A record crowd of 53,658 turned out to see if Broadway Joe would play.

He would. The veteran Taliaferro was unable to move the team, and in the second period Namath, wearing white shoes and a huge number 12 on his jersey back, ran onto the field. The quarterback worked quickly, hitting Maynard on his very first pro pass. He was 11 of 23 that day, for 121 yards and a touchdown, but the Jets lost, 14-10.

Ewbank wasn't so sure about Namath's skills—yet. He started Joe the next week, and the rookie threw for 287 yards and two touchdowns, but the Jets lost again. The following week he did not have any touchdowns against Denver and was 5 of 21 the week after that. Ewbank started Taliaferro again the next week.

Namath's early jitters were not due to a lack of talent but a lack of experience. "He just wasn't used to his new receivers. He knew where his boys at Alabama were going to be, but was not used to us," said one of his Jets receivers. "He'd throw short to one guy and too high to another. Everything was just a little off. After a few games, when we all got used to each other, he got better."

That was against the Kansas City Chiefs, one of the AFL's best teams. Namath came in when Taliaferro couldn't move the team, and he completed 7 of 16 for 81 yards and a touchdown in a win. He had poise, he had confidence, and his sharp bullet passes were neither short or long. His first full game was the next Sunday against the Houston Oilers. He hit 17 of 26 passes for 221 yards and four touchdowns. He had arrived. Namath would go on to be voted Rookie of the Year in the AFL. He wound up with 164 completions in 340 attempts for 2,220 yards and 18 touchdowns that year (with 15 interceptions) and was also the MVP in the AFL All-Star game.

Namath and Coach Weeb Ewbank survey the action during a practice. Ewbank's coaching innovations were geared to protecting his quarterback and allowing Namath extra chances of displaying his genius.

What made Namath so popular with fans was not his raw talent but his electricity and cockiness. Fans didn't resent his white shoes— they saw them as a symbol of super confidence. (Some writers called him "Willie White Shoes.") And he always played to win. New York had a history loving flashy players who win.

"Lots of young quarterbacks," said Don Maynard, "throw a lot of easy screen passes and five-yard-down-and-out sideline passes to put up the numbers. 'Joe Smith was 8 of 10 in the first half,' right? You see that a lot today, even with the big names. Put up the numbers. Joe never did that. He always threw for the first down. He'd force passes to get first downs. If we were inside the 20 yardline, all he wanted to do was throw into the end zone. He played to win the game, for nothing else."

And he won games. That rookie season, he took a lackluster Jets team to a 5-8-1 season, good for second place in their division. The five wins came in their last eight games, as the new quarterback began to mesh with his receivers. In 1966, in only his second season, he became one of the most dominant quarterbacks in the history of professional football. In complete control of his team's offense and calling virtually all of the plays, he filled the air with the football. Joe led the AFL in attempts (with 471), completions (232), yards (3,379), and touchdowns (19). He did throw 27 interceptions, an uncomfortably high number. The Jets' record improved to 6-6-2 (third place), and the flamboyant Joe, who backed up his cockiness with success, had become a New York hero and national sports figure.

He did much of it in excruciating pain, though. The knee was bothering him again. This time, to compensate for the pain in one knee, he put too much stress on the other and that one was starting to hurt. Near the end of the season, he played every game in great pain and at times could hardly walk. At least once a week, he had to have a needle drain his knee of fluid. Dr. James Nicholas, the Jets' physician, told him that if he didn't undergo another extensive knee operation, he would never play again.

"It was awful to see him limping around out there, his knee swelling, having to be drained constantly," said Nicholas.

Joe, by now used to knee operations, agreed, and Nicholas did a battery of tests right after the final game of the season. He had grim and startling news for Werblin and Ewbank. Namath did not have a sore knee or weak knee. Apparently, in the early part of the season, he had torn the cartilage in the knee, a major injury, and played the entire season on a shredded knee. Immediate surgery was necessary.

Again, the surgery was a success. Namath could begin 1967 with reasonably good knees (held intact with a large brace he had to wear each game). Joe got the healthy prognosis the same week that the first Super Bowl was held, a game which would figure prominently in his future and the future of all American sports.

The 1967 season was a landmark for Namath and for the AFL. Joe, looking like his own air force, put the ball in the sky constantly, leading the league with a record 491 attempts, record 258 completions, and record 4,007 yards, and 26 touchdowns in leading the Jets to a second-place finish and an 8-5-1 record despite injuries to running backs which probably cost them first place. He was the first

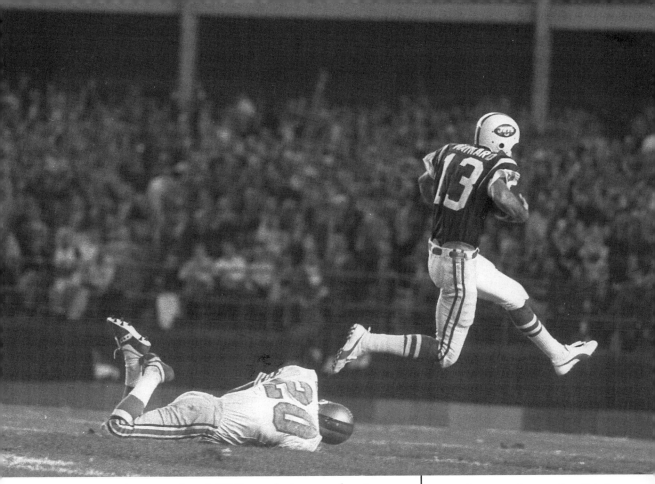

man ever to pass for 4,000 yards in any league.

Coach Ewbank was pleased with his quarterback's third season. "He's more experienced. He doesn't misread defenses any more," he said.

Coaches of other teams just shook their heads after Joe riddled their pass defenses on Sunday afternoons. "He's like a machine when he gets going," said Lou Saban of the Denver Broncos. "You've got to give him credit. He's a heckuva quarterback. He drives his team out on that field. He's tough and he keeps them in there all the time."

People in the NFL were taking notice, too. Roger LeClerc, veteran Chicago Bears linebacker, compared him to the two best quarterbacks of recent history. "I think Namath is a

Don Maynard was the Jets' premier deep threat and Namath's favorite target. Here he catches a bomb from Namath and bounds away from Houston's Miller Farr on his way to a touchdown.

better deep thrower than Bart Starr [of the Green Bay Packers] and he completes the quick ones like Johnny Unitas [of the Baltimore Colts]. And he recognizes the defenses the way both of them do."

Werblin and Ewbank slowly stocked the Jets with good ballplayers. Namath arrived with Maynard and Bake Turner in camp. Matt Snell and Emerson Boozer, two tough running backs, were signed. Werblin and Ewbank signed several top defensive backs. Top college stars, aware that increased TV exposure and growing fan support meant the AFL was permanent, turned their backs on the NFL and signed. Werblin's contract with Namath meant that other AFL teams were soon paying good salaries for their players. Slowly, the AFL was beating the NFL in signing college stars.

In 1967, Namath put up tremendous numbers, but in 1968 he showed he was not merely a great quarterback, he was also a real team leader. And thanks to Coach Ewbank, he had a team that played better as a unit than perhaps any team in the AFL.

"We really came together in 1968. No cliques, no friction, no resentment, all of us working like hell to win the championship," said Joe. "We were a group, we were together. That was the whole story of 1968, that was what made us champions—the unity we had, the confidence we all had in each other. Damn, we liked each other."

The players respected him. Maynard, the veteran receiver, admired Joe's openmindedness. "I played with 26 different quarterbacks in pro ball and he was the only one—the *only* one—who would listen to me when I suggested something a little different. For instance, many passes are never thrown because the pattern is busted. If the receiver isn't open or cuts some different way and the quarterback doesn't know where he's going, most quarterbacks eat the ball or throw it away. I told Joe early on, and Sauer and the others agreed, that if we just put together two part patterns we'd never have that problem. For example, if I couldn't get free on a sideline pattern, I could always cut back towards the hashmarks and go down 10 yards. He'd look, see I was trapped, wait half a second, and throw back and down 10 yards. In the 10 years I played with Joe Namath, in some 150 games, maybe 3,500 pass plays, we had a completely busted pattern exactly one time."

Maynard also admired Namath's willingness to listen. "He'd come to me and ask me what I wanted to do, the patterns I wanted to run, the things I wanted to try. He'd use them. If I told him I knew I could beat a guy deep, he'd throw to me deep. He listened and that's why he was so good."

5

"I GUARANTEE IT"

The Jets had a rocky preseason in 1968. But just before the season started, Namath was elected captain of the offense. He was startled and said it "was the greatest honor I've ever had."

The first game of the season was a tough but important win for the Jets. Leading by a single point, the Jets had the ball on their own four yardline. Namath engineered a brilliant, powerful drive to the Chiefs' 28, eating up six minutes on the clock and winning the game as time ran out. It proved they were smart and it proved they were not going to fold late in the game, as they had several times in previous years.

The Jets pounded the Boston Patriots the next week, 47-31, then lost a close one to the Buffalo Bills, 37-35, in which Namath threw

Carleton Oats of the Oakland Raiders (number 85) is about to crunch Namath in the famous "Heidi" game of 1968. The Jets were winning with just over a minute left to play, but the Raiders came back to win—while fans at home were left to watch a movie instead of the exciting finale.

three interceptions which went for touchdowns. They bounced back the next week. In another close one, they came from behind to beat the San Diego Chargers, 23-20.

The Jets then lost to a lightly regarded Broncos team, 21-13, and Namath was depressed. The usually glib Broadway Joe hung his head low in the lockerroom. "Just say I stink. I really stink," he told the reporters and turned his back.

A few days after the Denver loss, Verlon Biggs turned up at Shea with a goatee. He told friends he wouldn't shave it off until the Jets had won the AFL title. The idea caught on, and soon everybody on the Jets started growing goatees and mustaches. Joe Namath, always the flamboyant one, decided on a scary Fu Manchu moustache which dripped down around the sides of his mouth.

The silly idea served to bind the players together. The Jets beat Houston the following week and Buffalo the week after that. In four straight games, Namath did not complete a touchdown pass. He didn't have to. Throughout the season, Weeb Ewbank implemented a beautifully balanced attack. With Snell and Boozer picking up needed rushing yardage game after game, Joe didn't have to throw on every other down. Namath's passes in 1968 dropped to 380 from 491 the year before and his total yardage went down to 3,147 from 4,007. His touchdown total dropped from 26 to 15. He didn't have to produce all by himself, just direct and make the big plays. And it didn't hurt that the Jets' defense would wind up leading the AFL.

Weeb Ewbank applied psychological pressure to motivate the team. One day, he posted a blown-up copy of a $25,000 check that players received for winning the Super Bowl on the bulletin board. On another, he posted a blown-up newspaper article with the headline: "Will The Jets Blow It Again?"

The Houston victory put the Jets back on the winning track, and wins over Boston, Buffalo, and Houston again followed. Then the team flew to California for their annual West Coast trip and a collision with the fierce Oakland Raiders.

The game was an offensive classic, with both teams battling back from deficits time after time. With just 65 seconds left in the more than three-hour-long game, the Jets held a 32-29 lead. The game had run so late, though, that it was cutting into a scheduled NBC-TV movie, "Heidi." Some middle manager at NBC, convinced nothing would happen in the last 65 seconds, pulled a switch and the game disappeared, and suddenly there was little Heidi romping through the Alps with her grandfather. Jet fans assumed the game had somehow ended and rejoiced. Within minutes, radios let football fans know from coast to coast that in the last harrowing 65 seconds the Raiders had scored not one but two touchdowns for a stunning 43-32 victory. NBC was deluged with tens of thousands of phone calls from irate fans.

The wild loss to the Raiders at first demoralized the Jets. But by the end of the week, as they prepared for another West Coast game in San Diego, the players' attitudes improved. From the wreckage of the Raider game they also resolved someday, somehow, to get even with Oakland. They got out all their pent-up frustrations and emotions and exploded in San Diego, with Broadway Joe back in top form. He threw for two touchdowns in a 37-15 runaway. The next week, the Jets won the division title and, a few days later, the players began shaving off their beards and mustaches, as promised.

And Broadway Joe and his Fu Manchu? He waited until a razor blade company offered him $15,000 and then shaved it off on their television commercial.

The Jets were determined to avoid the late season letdown that winning a division title early might cause. Namath, alternating at quarterback with veteran Babe Parilli, led the Jets to three straight wins. The east division champs were ready to take on the west division champs for the AFL championship, and they were none other than the silver and black desperadoes of pro football, the Raiders.

This time the Jets didn't have to fly anywhere. The title game was at Shea Stadium. Weather conditions were marvelous—freezing cold. That was the first advantage the Jets had over the fair weather boys from California. The second was a roaring home crowd of 62,627 New Yorkers, the largest title game crowd in AFL history. The third was Joe Namath, a quarterback determined to get revenge on the Raiders for the Heidi loss and determined to bring New York an AFL title and take the Jets to the Super Bowl.

The Jets started out flying. Namath hit Maynard with a 14-yard touchdown pass to put the Jets ahead 7-0 after just three minutes. The Jets added a field goal. Then Fred Biletnikoff, the sure-handed Oakland receiver, hauled in a 29-yard touchdown pass from Daryle Lamonica. Right after that, Raider linemen Ben Davidson

Namath's Fu Manchu mustache made him look fierce, but he shaved it off at the behest of a razor company. Later in his career, he made another famous ad wearing pantyhose.

and Isaac Lassiter broke blocks and converged on Namath, one high and one low, and slammed his body onto the frozen turf. Joe, who had bruised his back early in the season, pushed his hand behind his back to ease the blow. But he fell the wrong way, dislocating the finger on his left hand and jamming the thumb on his throwing hand. Instead of sitting down for the rest of the day, he told the trainer just to tape the finger to a piece of board and give his thumb a hard yank. Then he trotted back to the field. A few minutes later, with 10 seconds left in the half, and the Jets holding a 13-10 lead, he was slammed to the turf again. He got up, dusted himself off, and trotted off the field and to the lockerroom.

In the lockerroom, Namath walked strangely, and the players were frightened. He didn't seem to have any idea where he was. Doctors and trainers rushed him into another room and emerged to tell Ewbank to get Parilli ready. Namath probably would not play again that day. Broadway Joe came out a moment later, shrugged off the doctors' advice, and talked Ewbank into letting him continue. The quarterback now had his usual bad knees, a dislocated finger, jammed thumb, bad back, and, to boot, throbbing headaches and dizziness.

He went back into the game.

The Raiders, fighting the Jets in the cold for every inch of the Shea Stadium turf, soon tied the game at 13-13 and later led, 23-20. The Jets got the ball back and the crowd held its breath, recognizing how great a game they were watching. Namath hit George Sauer on the left for 10 yards, then dropped back and arched a gorgeous 52-yard-pass to Maynard that brought

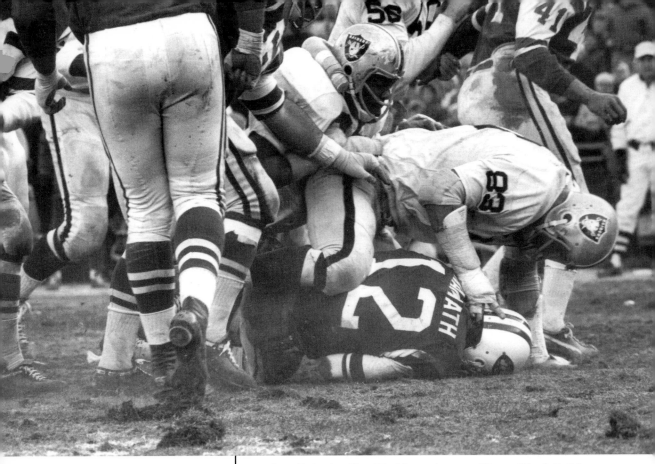

Oakland's Ben Davidson squashed Namath several times in the playoff rematch of the Heidi game. But the Jets prevailed and won the right to play the Baltimore Colts in the 1969 Super Bowl.

the Jets to the Raider six yardline. He hit Maynard again for a touchdown and a 27-23 win and the Jets' first AFL championship.

The honors rolled in for Namath: AFL Player of the Year, George Halas Award as Most Courageous Player (for coming back with his bad knees), quarterback on every AFL all-star team selected and many AFL teams. But there was one more game to be played.

Against all expectations, the Jets dominated the Super Bowl, thanks to Namath's inspired leadership. At the end of the game, Namath led his Jets running off the field toward the lockerroom. He held his forefinger high in the air to signal the Jets were Number One. Celebrations in New York lasted into the wee hours of the morning.

The Jets' locker room was full of shouting and yelling. Pete Rozelle, the NFL commissioner, walked in to congratulate the team, and someone yelled out: "Hey Pete, welcome to the AFL!" The boys roared.

Looking back on that game, Namath was pleased. "I had a good game," he said, analyzing Super Bowl III. "I didn't throw into coverage. I didn't call anything to the wrong side of the defense. But most of all, it was a total team victory. I can't think of a player on our team who played a mediocre game. Hey, Matt Snell running over all those guys. Al Atkinson, our middle linebacker, playing with a separated shoulder and reaching up to tip away a pass at the goal line. Dave Herman switching over to tackle and having a great game against Bubba..."

And he thought, too, that emotion was riding with the Jets and all their fans. "There are a lot of underdogs out there in the world, in our country," he said. "They'd seen the AFL lose in the first two Super Bowls. Now it was our turn to be heavy underdogs. But we played 60 minutes and won, and maybe that meant something to all those people out there who felt they were underdogs....I can't tell you how many [high school and college] coaches told me afterward that they used our game as a motivator. But maybe it meant something to the underdogs in life, too."

Months later, after many people told him that if Baltimore had done certain things differently and the Jets had done certain things differently, the outcome would have been different, Namath watched the game film again.

"They were all right," he said. "If things had gone a little differently, we would have beaten Baltimore much worse."

Namath's Super Bowl performance impressed everybody. He was named pro football player of the year and won the prestigious Hickock Belt for athlete of the year. By the end of spring, his apartment had filled up with trophies, certificates, and citations. He was hired for television commercials and was a sought-after speaker for luncheons, dinners, and receptions. Back in New York, as he returned to the club scene, Broadway Joe was bigger than ever. He and his teammates were given a tickertape parade down—where else?—Broadway.

He won the respect of everyone, including the Colts he had fired up so often. The same sportswriters who made fun of Joe's Super Bowl prediction trotted out his amazing statistics for his first four years: 1,632 attempts, 841 comple-

---

Six months after the Super Bowl, Namath quit football when NFL Commissioner Pete Rozelle demanded Namath sell his interest in a night club. Fortunately, Namath unretired in time for the regular season. (That's sportscaster Howard Cosell at the far right.)

tions, 13,330 yards, and 78 touchdowns, and an astounding average of 7.7 yards per pass attempt.

"He was all we had heard, a fine football player," said Colt coach Don Shula.

"He did it all. He threw the ball short a little. He threw the ball long a little. He ran the ball a little. He had it all going and so they won," said Colt lineman Billy Ray Smith.

John Mackey, who played against just about every top quarterback in his long career, always admired Namath. "Everybody paid attention to his arm and the passing, but if you study his career, you see that he was a skilled playmaker. Most coaches send in all the plays. Joe called his own plays. He'd call many of his plays at the line. He had a nice balance of running and passing. Many times he would go for the run if the opponent had a weak line, reducing his own passing numbers. He did what it took for the team to win. People forget that."

Even the former great quarterbacks, who bristled at his bragging, joined the Namath camp.

"He could go down as the best passer who ever played," said "Slinging" Sammy Baugh, the great Washington Redskins quarterback of the 1930s and 1940s. "He's the fastest on his feet I have ever seen."

"He can really wing that ball in there. He has strength and accuracy and you'd better get to him or he will run you out of the park. He is in a class by himself," said Paul Brown, longtime coach of the Cleveland Browns.

The most important achievement of Joe Namath in the Super Bowl was to put the entire AFL on the same level with the NFL. The years of arguments by league officials and players were nowhere near as effective as the 60 minutes of football and the predictions of Joe Namath. Super Bowl III proved to one and all that the leagues were equal. It spurred the drive to create one permanent football league. The AFL and NFL played separate seasons in 1969, but beginning in 1970 the AFL and NFL merged into one giant NFL. The Jets were placed in the AFC East Division.

Spring and summer went by quietly for Namath as he made his speech engagements, signed his endorsement deals, and appeared for his commercials. Then, without warning, he once again found himself at the center of a firestorm of controversy that threatened to end his career.

Namath, the night owl, had become partners with friends in a New York night club called Bachelors III. In June 1969, NFL Commissioner Pete Rozelle called Namath to his office and told him that the league had been investigating Bachelors III and had found that a number of professional gamblers, men who reportedly bet heavily on professional football, hung out there. Namath had done nothing wrong. No one accused him of betting on games or discussing point spreads on games with gamblers. Neither of his partners had done anything wrong. Yet Rozelle insisted that Namath sell his interest in the club because his ownership gave the appearance of consorting with gamblers.

Joe refused. He insisted that lots of people came in and out of the club and he really had no idea who they were or what they did. Rozelle was angry, though, and finally told Namath that he had to choose between the nightclub and football. A tearful Namath held a press conference in late June and said the issue had gone beyond the club and betting and had become an issue of his honor and his reputation. It was also a matter of friendship. People came to the club because Joe owned part of it and hung out there. People came in hoping they might spot him and talk to him or get an autograph. Without him, the club might go out of business, and his two friends might lose a lot of money. Namath, torn inside, stunned the sports world and announced he was quitting football.

The controversy raged throughout the summer, and the fans took sides. Most sided with Joe. Finally, tired of lawyers and headlines, Joe settled the issue by selling his interest in the bar the next spring. Meanwhile, he reported to camp right on time for the 1969 season.

Namath was sharp again as preseason training opened that summer. He had another great season in 1969, completing 185 of 361 passes for 2,734 yards and 19 touchdowns. He led the Jets to another division title, with a 10-4 record, but they fell to the Kansas City Chiefs in the AFL title game. The Chiefs went on to win Super Bowl IV, the second straight AFL victory, which hurried the merger of the leagues.

It was a year, like all years, in which Namath not only battled the defensive backfield of pro football but battled his knees. "I never played a down of pro football with a good knee. My game was left in college," Namath said later. "Dr. Nicholas of the Jets didn't see my knee until I'd hurt it for the fifth time. I'd had it go out and ripped up five times before he operated on it the first time. I kept tearing it up at Alabama. But I still had some mobility, until I tore two hamstring muscles waterskiing. That was awful. My last six or seven years in the

NFL, I could take one stride setting up, then maybe a second one, then I'd be breaking down by the fourth."

Teammates who knew how difficult it was for a normal quarterback to play pro football, with all the hits and sacks, marvelled at Joe's ability to play with pain.

It wasn't his knees that wrecked the 1970 season, though. It was his wrist. After a fine start in 1970, Joe went down hard on a sack, and as soon as his body hit the dirt he felt a searing pain in his wrist. The injury ruined his entire season. He kept telling the press he hoped it would heal, but it did not, and he missed the last nine games. Without Joe, the Jets fell apart, winning just four and losing 10. The wrist didn't bother him in 1971, but his knee went out again. Joe missed another 10 games, and the Jets finished 6-8.

Namath had the beautiful Ann-Margret as his co-star in C. C. and Company. She went on to have a major movie career. He didn't.

Joe knew that his injuries would cut short his career, as health problems had plagued so many other football players. (In fact, he would have both knees replaced two decades later.) Friends urged him to make as much money as he could doing commercials, which he did. In 1970, during the offseason, Joe made his first movie, *C.C. and Company.* Two years later, he tried television, starring in a series called "Waverly Wonders," which lasted only one season. Later, when his career was over, he spent several

As Namath's health got worse, so did the New York Jets. The team won three and lost 11 during each of the last two years he played with them.

years traveling around the country starring in musical plays, such as "Damn Yankees," "Guys and Dolls," "Bells Are Ringing" and "Sugar." He tackled difficult roles, too, starring in "The Caine Mutiny" on Broadway.

Joe's acting did not overly impress critics, but it pleased audiences. To the public, Broadway Joe would always be a star, no matter where they saw him. His theater appearances drew large audiences, and every night after the show dozens of people would wait for him to say hello and get autographs or have their pictures taken with him.

"I've never seen anything like the audience reaction to him. When a true theater star walks on stage for the first time, the audience gives him or her a polite round of applause. When Joe stepped on to the stage, the audience stood up and cheered. People where whistling at him, yelling 'way to go Joe.' It was just like at a football stadium when he trotted into the first huddle of the game," said Glenn Lillie, vice president of the Claridge Hotel, where Namath starred in two musicals in the mid 1980s. "I think someone like him has that rare star quality about him. It doesn't matter what he does, he's a star and people react to him that way."

He worked just as hard at being a good actor as he did being a good quarterback. Maynard Sloate, who directed him in several plays, thought he worked as hard, or harder, than anybody else in show business.

"He was never a prima donna. He was always on time. He listened to advice from producers, directors and other actors. He studied his scenes and lines. He even, on his own, hired a vocal coach to work with him to improve his speech and singing," said Sloate. "He was so good in 'Sugar' on the East Coast that he was asked to star in another production of it on the West Coast."

Sloate, who lives in Las Vegas, knew nothing of the cocky image Namath had in the New York press. When told of it later, he was surprised. "I found Joe Namath to be a down to earth, very modest man. Quite nice. Not a bit of ego in him. I wish all actors I work with were like Joe Namath," Sloate said.

In 1972, fans wondered if Joe was finished. Few players in any sport had rebounded after missing most of two seasons to two serious injuries. Would the chronically weak knees hold up?

Joe reported to training camp and told everyone he was as healthy as any time in his career. His ever loyal players let him know they were behind him in camp, once again electing him captain of the offensive unit. (He told them to pick someone else in 1971 because of his injuries.) He had the complete support of the owners and coaches, too.

In 1972, Joe Namath, playing with an all-new set of braces on his legs, put together one of the best seasons of any quarterback in pro football history. He passed for 496 yards and six touchdowns in one game against the Baltimore Colts and 403 yards in another against the Oakland Raiders. (Don Maynard's seven receptions broke Raymond Berry's career reception record.) It would be only the third time in history a quarterback had two 400-yard games in one year. He also passed for 301 yards against Houston in the Astrodome. After these weekly passing displays, he then tripped up a Patriots team determined to stop his aerial attack by converting the Jets to a running offense, working with John Riggins and Emerson Boozer to produce 333 rushing yards, a team record. By the end of the year, Joe had thrown 324 passes, completing 162 of them for a league-leading 2,816 yards and a league-leading 19 touchdowns. He made All Pro again and led the Jets to a second-place finish in their division.

In 1973, the knees were okay and the wrist was fine, but in the sixth game of the year, determined to tackle an opposing player who had picked up a fumble, Namath separated his shoulder. He missed the rest of the year.

Hard luck Joe, who never even considered quitting after losing most of three seasons to injury, went back into training in the spring of 1974 and was back in shape by September. Injury free, he had another great year, completing 191 of 361 for 2,616 yards and 20 touchdowns. He threw too many interceptions, a league-leading 22, though defenders argued that many were not his fault. In 1975, he hit nearly half his passes for 2,285 yards and 15 touchdowns. Again, forcing some passes and underthrowing others, he led the league in interceptions with a dangerous 28. Although he had good statistics, he was not winning. The Jets, now without many of their stars of the late 1960s, finished a weak 3-11 that year.

In 1976, Joe's numbers slipped. He started 11 games but only threw 230 times, hitting 49.6 percent but for just 1,090 yards, a poor average of only four yards per pass attempt. Fifteen passes were intercepted. The Jets were again a grim 3 wins, 11 losses. Under Namath's leadership, the Jets, once World Champions and the toast of New York, finished fourth in their division in 1973, third in 1974, fourth in 1975, and fourth again in 1976. There may have been a million lights on Broadway that year, as the saying goes, but few were lighting up for Broadway Joe.

On April's Fools Day, 1977, Joe left Broadway for good. After an extremely disappointing 1976 season, the $500,000-a-year quarterback was put on waivers. That meant the Jets didn't want him and any NFL team could have him if they were willing to match the $500,000 salary (plus 10 percent). The 10-day waiver period went by, but no team claimed him. The NFL routinely then asked the Jets if they wanted Joe back, and they said no. Broadway Joe's reign in

New York was over, and nobody wanted him.

Then a call came from the Los Angeles Rams. If Namath was willing to take a huge pay cut, down to just $150,000 a year, and willing to undergo an extensive preseason training program, the Rams would give him a chance. The front office was high on Joe Namath as a gate attraction and as a high-profile player who might provide the leadership the talented team needed. The players, who had followed Namath's up-and-down career for years, agreed.

"Joe Namath is here to provide the spark which will make us a Super Bowl team," said linebacker Isaiah Robertson.

Fans and sportswriters in Los Angeles, although frustrated by the constant near misses at titles for the Rams, weren't so sure Broadway Joe could become Freeway Joe. After all, didn't the Rams have a very capable quarterback in young, strong, and smart Pat Haden, the Rhodes Scholar out of the University of South California, a local hero who had done very well in his first year at the helm? His backup was James Harris, another young, strong, and injury-free signal caller. Why not build for the future instead of reaching back to the past? The 1969 Super Bowl victory, great as it was, happened a long time ago. A quick poll of southern California sportswriters was ominous. Of 38 writers polled, 36 said Joe should not have been signed.

A smiling Namath arrived in Los Angeles early for training and paid no attention to the doubts of the writers or fans. He told everybody he was just trying to make the team and would do whatever he had to do to wind up as the Rams' number one quarterback. He was very serious about it, as serious as anything in his life.

Namath felt he could still play and the warm weather of Los Angeles would help him do that (cold weather always bothered his knees). He wanted to get back into the Super Bowl again, and the well-stocked Rams of 1977 were a team with promise. Also, it must have occurred to him that a good way of extending his Hollywood career was to star in front of all the L.A. television and movie producers.

Namath arrived in Los Angeles at just 187 pounds, 20 pounds below his rather pudgy 1976 playing weight. He had taken off the pounds, but not the trimness or muscle, on his own. He worked with Rams' trainers and doctors to get himself into even better shape. Since he couldn't participate in running programs with his knees and braces, they devised a swimming program for him which helped. By the time the exhibition season started, he was ready for the NFL once again—possibly in better shape than at any time since the late 1960s.

Time was not on Namath's side anymore, though. The years had taken their toll on his mobility and agility. Pat Haden, the good-looking, clean-cut, clean-living, happily-married All-American, got the nod as quarterback when the season began. Haden had quarterbacked the team the year before, in his rookie season, and had also finished his classes at Oxford University in England. (He spent six months in each country).

Haden was gracious in the competition between the two quarterbacks. "Before I left for England I was told that anybody they brought in would have to beat me out," he said. "I thought to myself that I'd rather have Joe Namath here than a lot of other people. I knew I could learn

Joe Namath poses with his bust after induction into the Pro Football Hall of Fame in 1985. Larry Bruno, left, was Namath's football coach at Beaver Falls, PA.

from him and I also knew that he wouldn't be playing forever."

Haden had a good year, leading the Rams to a 10-4 record and the division title. Namath spent most of the year on the bench. His knees hurt every day. He only got into six games. He attempted 107 passes, completing 50 for three touchdowns. At the end of the year, knowing he should put no more stress on his aching body, Joe Namath retired from football. He soon began a second career as a broadcaster.

The statistics for his 13-year-career earned Namath easy election to the Pro Football Hall of Fame in 1985. He played in 143 games, attempted 3,762 passes, completing 1,886 of them (50.6 percent) for 27,663 yards and 173 touchdowns. At the time of his retirement, he had set many records, though all were later broken by other quarterbacks. At one point he was in the record books for most passes attempted in one game (62), most consecutive passes completed (15), most 300-passing-yard games in a season (6), most touchdown passes as a rookie (18), and most passing yards gained in one game (496). The kid from Beaver Falls who was too small to get into most of his high school games did all right.

JOE NAMATH:
A CHRONOLOGY

1943   Born, May 31, in Beaver Falls, Pennsylvania.

1960   Quarterbacks his high school team to an undefeated season; accepts a scholarship to the University of Alabama.

1962   Leads Alabama to a victory in the Orange Bowl.

1964   Injures his knee in a game against North Carolina State University; Alabama loses to the University of Texas in the Orange Bowl.

1965   Drafted in the first round by the New York Jets of the AFL; is signed for a record salary at that time; is named Rookie of the Year in the AFL and MVP in the AFL All-Star Game.

1967   Leads the league in passing attempts, completions, and yards gained for second year in a row; also leads league in average gain per pass attempt (8.2); named to AFL All-Star Game.

1968   Leads Jets to 11-3 record and AFL Championship; is named Sporting News AFL Player of the Year.

1969   Jets defeat Baltimore Colts in Super Bowl III, one of the great upsets in sports history.

1972   Leads league in passing yardage and touchdowns thrown; named to Pro Bowl.

1977   Is released by New York Jets; signs as free agent with Los Angeles Rams; retires at end of season and becomes a broadcaster.

1985   Inducted into the Pro Football Hall of Fame.

STATISTICS

JOSEPH WILLIAM NAMATH

YEAR	TEAM	G	ATT	CMP	PCT	YDS	TD	INT
1965	NY Jets	14	340	164	48.2	2220	13	15
1966	NY Jets	14	**471**	**232**	49.3	**3379**	**19**	**27**
1967	NY Jets	14	**491**	**258**	52.5	**4007**	**26**	**28**
1968	NY Jets	14	380	187	49.2	3147	15	17
1969	NY Jets	14	361	185	51.2	2734	19	17
1970	NY Jets	5	179	90	50.3	1259	5	12
1971	NY Jets	4	59	28	47.5	537	5	6
1972	NY Jets	13	324	162	50.0	**2816**	**19**	21
1973	NY Jets	6	133	68	51.1	966	5	6
1974	NY Jets	14	361	191	52.9	2616	20	**22**
1975	NY Jets	14	326	157	43.2	2285	15	**28**
1976	NY Jets	11	230	114	49.6	1090	4	16
1977	LA Rams	6	107	50	46.7	606	3	5
TOTALS		143	3,762	1,886	50.1	27,663	173	220

G	games
ATT	attempts
CMP	completions
PCT	percent
YDS	yards
TD	touchdowns
INT	interceptions

Bold indicates league-leading statistics

SUGGESTIONS FOR FURTHER READING

Allen, George, and Bob Olan. *Pro Football's Greatest Players*. New York: Bobbs-Merrill & Co., 1982.

Allen, Maury. *Joe Namath's Sportin' Life*. New York: Paperback Library, 1969.

Berger, Phil. *Joe Namath: Maverick Quarterback*. New York, Cowles Book Co., 1969.

Borstein, Larry. *Super Joe: The Joe Namath Story*. New York: Grosset & Dunlap, 1969.

Coffey, Wayne. *All Pro's Greatest Football Players*. New York: Scholastic Books, 1983.

Fox, Larry. *Broadway Joe and His Super Jets*. New York: Coward-McCann, Inc., 1969.

Herskowitz, Mickey. *The Legend of Bear Bryant*. New York: McGraw-Hill, Inc., 1987.

Lipman, David. *Joe Namath*. New York: G. P. Putnam's Sons, 1968.

Namath, Joe, with Dick Schaap. *I Can't Wait Until Tomorrow...'Cause I Get Better Looking Every Day*. New York: Random House, 1969.

Telander, Rick. *Joe Namath and the Other Guys*. New York: Holt, Rinehart & Winston, 1976.

ABOUT THE AUTHOR

Bruce Chadwick, a longtime columnist with the *New York Daily News*, has written over 300 magazine articles, 11 nonfiction books, and one novel. Among his books are *When the Game Was Black and White, American Summers: Minor League Baseball,* and *How to Buy, Trade and Invest in Baseball Cards and Collectibles* (written with Danny Peary). Chadwick teaches writing at New York University and is an associate resident fellow at the Smithsonian, where he lectures on baseball's role in American society.

INDEX

PICTURE CREDITS
UPI/Bettmann: pp. 2, 10, 12, 15, 22, 25, 28, 32, 34, 37, 40, 46, 48, 54, 60; AP/Wide World Photos: pp. 8, 44; Resource and Research Center for Beaver County and Local History, Beaver Falls, PA: pp. 16, 19, 20